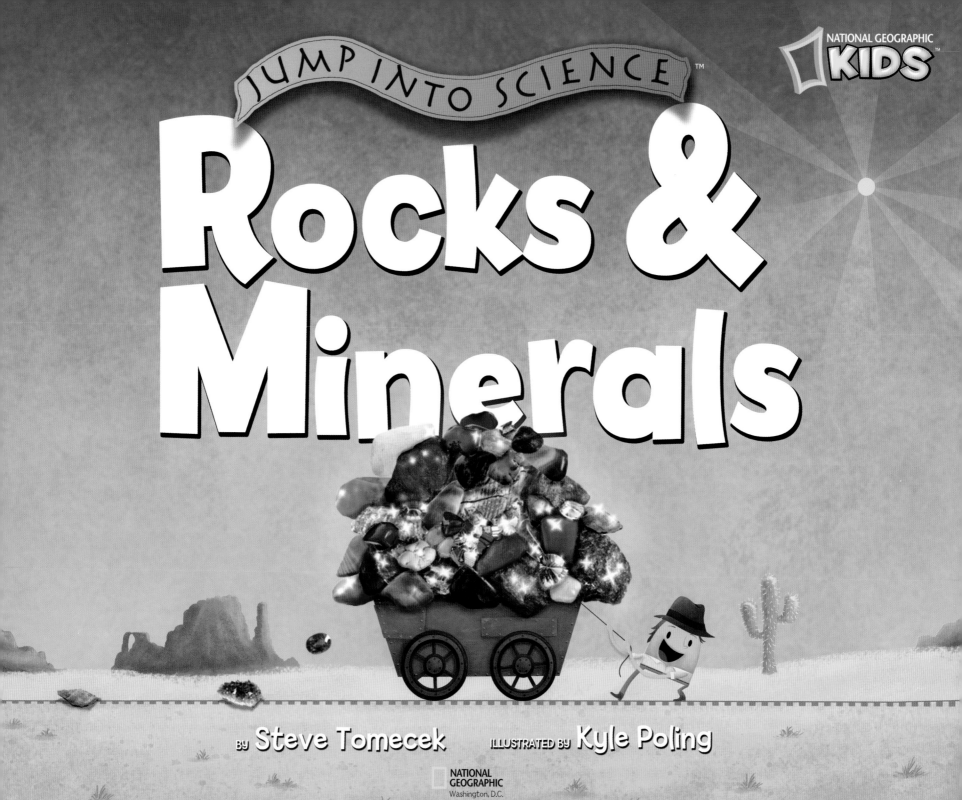

JUMP INTO SCIENCE™

NATIONAL GEOGRAPHIC
KIDS™

Rocks & Minerals

BY **Steve Tomecek**   ILLUSTRATED BY **Kyle Poling**

NATIONAL
GEOGRAPHIC
Washington, D.C.

Dedications

In memory of my dear friend
Dr. Walter S. Newman, a great scientist
who inspired me to become a geologist and
who taught me how to "read the rocks."
—S.T.

For my Mom and Dad and art teacher, Suzie.
I can't thank you enough for your love,
encouragement, support, and pushing me
to follow my dreams.
—K.P.

Rocks are all around us. Have you ever wondered where all these rocks come from? What are rocks made of? Here's your chance to become a "rock star" and discover the wonderful world of rocks!

The First Rocks

Scientists who study rocks are called geologists. Most geologists believe that the first rocks here on Earth formed more than 4.5 billion (4,500,000,000) years ago!

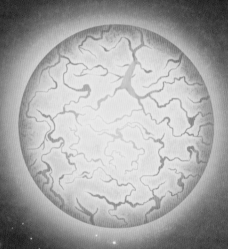

Geologists think that in the beginning, our Earth started as a big ball of super hot dust and gas.

As the planet cooled, the gas turned into a liquid called magma.

Later the magma cooled to make solid rocks.

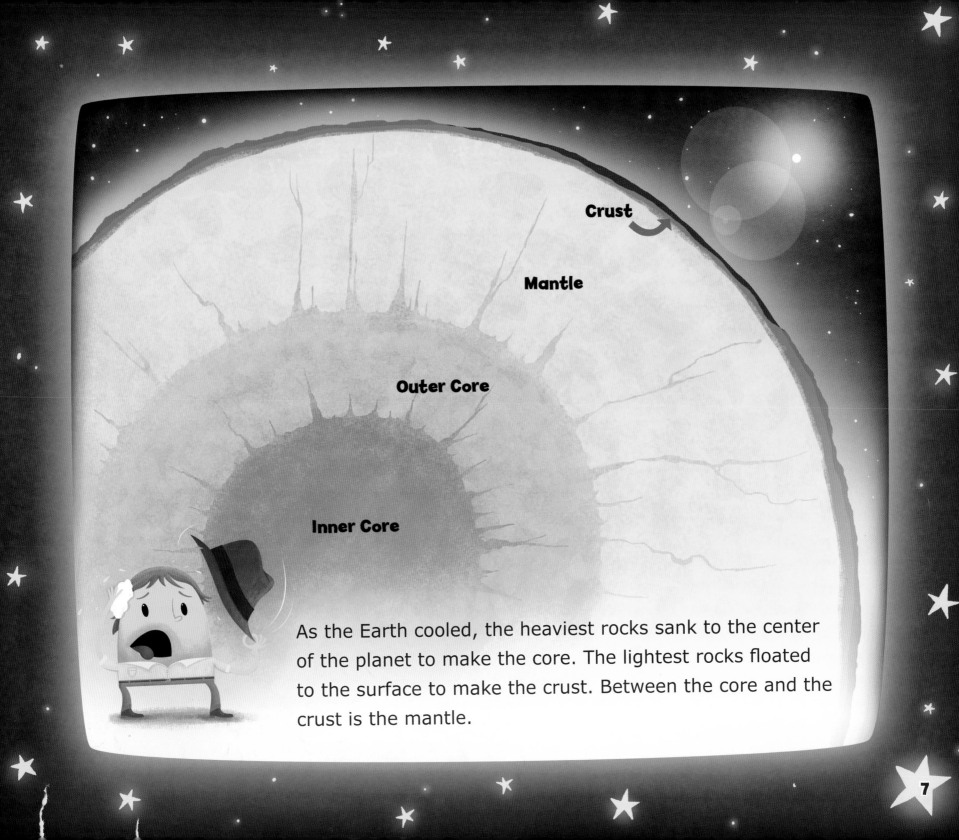

Crust

Mantle

Outer Core

Inner Core

As the Earth cooled, the heaviest rocks sank to the center of the planet to make the core. The lightest rocks floated to the surface to make the crust. Between the core and the crust is the mantle.

The Building Blocks of Rocks

Almost all rocks are made of tiny "building blocks" called minerals. Most minerals have their own special shape called a crystal. Some rocks are made from only one type of mineral, while others have many different minerals joined together.

Calcite

Garnet

Mica

Sapphire

Jade

Amethyst

Copper

Geologists have discovered more than 2,500 different minerals on our planet. Each mineral has its own special properties. A property is something that scientists use to describe an object. Some mineral properties include the shape of the crystal, its color, how hard it is, and how it shines. Some minerals are used to make jewelry and for decorations. These special minerals are called gems.

Emerald

Diamond

Salt

Quartz

Iron Pyrite

Snow Crystal

How Rocks Are Used

Over time, people discovered that rocks could be used for many different purposes. Thousands of years ago people used rocks to make tools such as arrowheads and scrapers.

Spear point

Scraper

Arrowheads

Notre-Dame Cathedral
Paris, France

Stonehenge
Galway Plain, England

Pantheon
Rome, Italy

In the past, rocks were also used for making great buildings. The pyramids in Egypt are made from rock. The ancient Greeks and Romans also built with rock. People are still using rocks in buildings. Is any part of your home made from rock?

How Rocks Form

Minerals don't just magically come together to make rocks. Rocks can only form when the conditions are right. After many years of studying different rocks, geologists discovered that rocks form in three main ways.

Granite

Igneous rock

Gneiss

Metamorphic rock

Geologists use the way a rock forms to put it into one of three different groups or types. The three main types of rock are called *igneous, metamorphic, and sedimentary.*

Conglomerate

Sedimentary rock

Igneous Rocks

Igneous rocks form as hot liquid rock, called magma, cools off. If the magma cools slowly, the rocks often form large crystals. If the magma cools quickly, crystals do not usually form. How fast the magma cools usually depends on whether the igneous rocks form deep underground or at the Earth's surface.

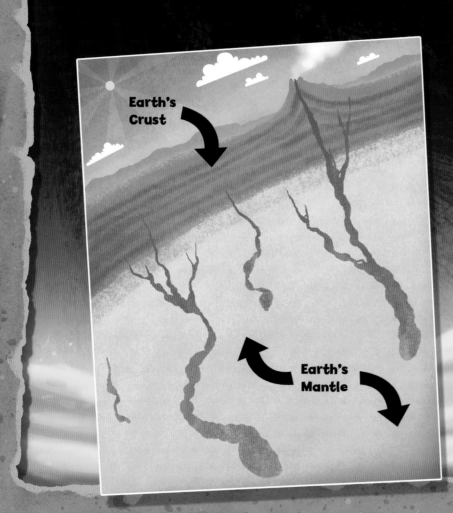

Earth's Crust

Earth's Mantle

When hot magma cools underground, it usually does so slowly. Igneous rocks that form inside the Earth often have large crystals. Granite and gabbro are two types of igneous rocks that form underground.

Granite

Gabbro

Magma

Lava

When hot magma reaches the surface of the Earth, geologists call it lava. Unlike magma inside the Earth, lava cools quickly so large crystals don't form. As the lava cools, it makes hills and mountains called volcanoes. These form on the surface of the Earth

Basalt

and can also form under water. The most common rock in the world is called basalt, and it forms from lava. Basalt is the type of rock that makes up most of the Earth's crust under the ocean.

Metamorphic Rocks

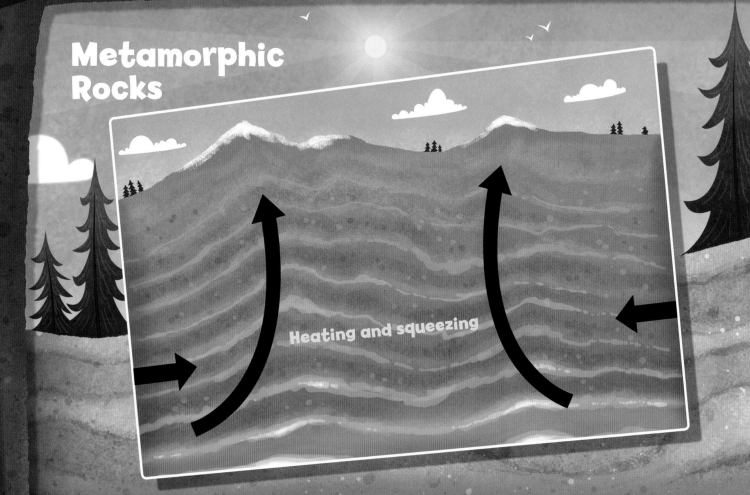

Heating and squeezing

A second type of rock is called metamorphic rock. Metamorphic rocks are rocks that have changed their form. Metamorphic rocks usually form deep inside the Earth where they get heated and squeezed by the rocks around them. Sometimes, metamorphic rocks have their minerals squeezed so much that they look like they came out of a tube of toothpaste!

Gneiss

Schist

The minerals in some metamorphic rocks look like they have flowed. They never turn back into liquid though. Instead they stretch and bend like warm clay. Two common metamorphic rocks are gneiss (pronounced nice) and schist (rhymes with twist).

Geologists have discovered that the crust of the Earth is not one solid piece. Instead it is made up of separate "chunks" called tectonic plates. These tectonic plates move slowly. When tectonic plates move, they squeeze the rocks around them.

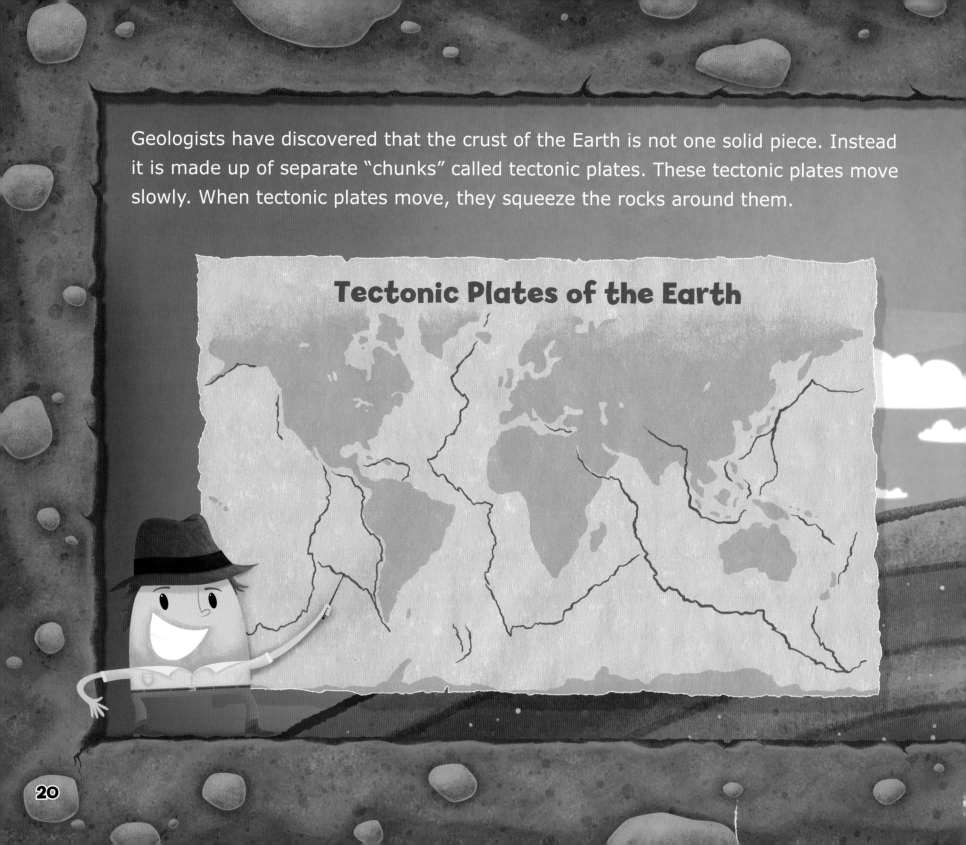

Tectonic Plates of the Earth

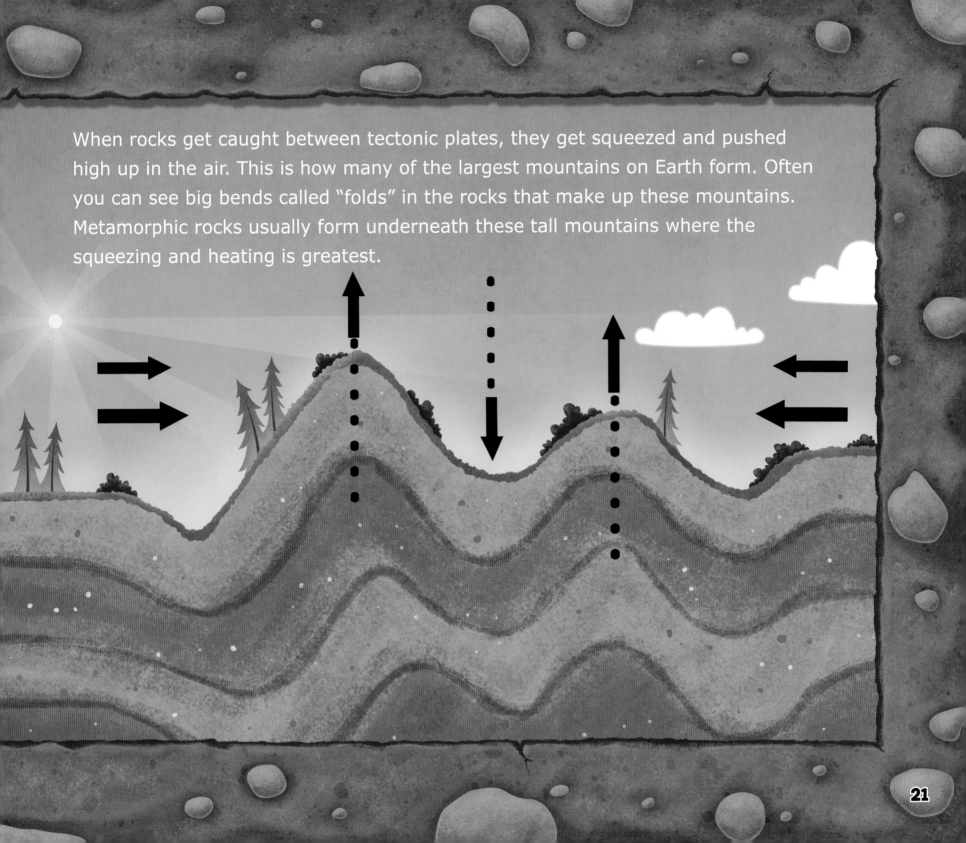

When rocks get caught between tectonic plates, they get squeezed and pushed high up in the air. This is how many of the largest mountains on Earth form. Often you can see big bends called "folds" in the rocks that make up these mountains. Metamorphic rocks usually form underneath these tall mountains where the squeezing and heating is greatest.

Sedimentary Rocks

The third major type of rock is called sedimentary rock. Sediment is another name for tiny pieces of rock that have broken off from larger rocks. Sand grains, pebbles, and mud are all different sizes of sediment. Sediment is created when wind, water, and ice wear down the rocks at the surface of the Earth.

Sediment is carried by rivers and streams to lakes and oceans where it begins to collect. Over time, the sediment piles up deeper and deeper. Layers at the bottom of the pile slowly get turned back into solid rock again.

Not all sedimentary rocks have grains in them. Some form from crystals that grow in water. As water flows over rocks, some of the minerals seem to disappear. Scientists say that the minerals dissolve. When the water with the dissolved minerals begins to dry up, or evaporate, new mineral crystals begin to form in it. Sedimentary rocks that form this way are called evaporites.

Try this!

Add salt to water and stir with a spoon so it all dissolves.

Allow the water to evaporate.

And look what you've got!

Salt again!

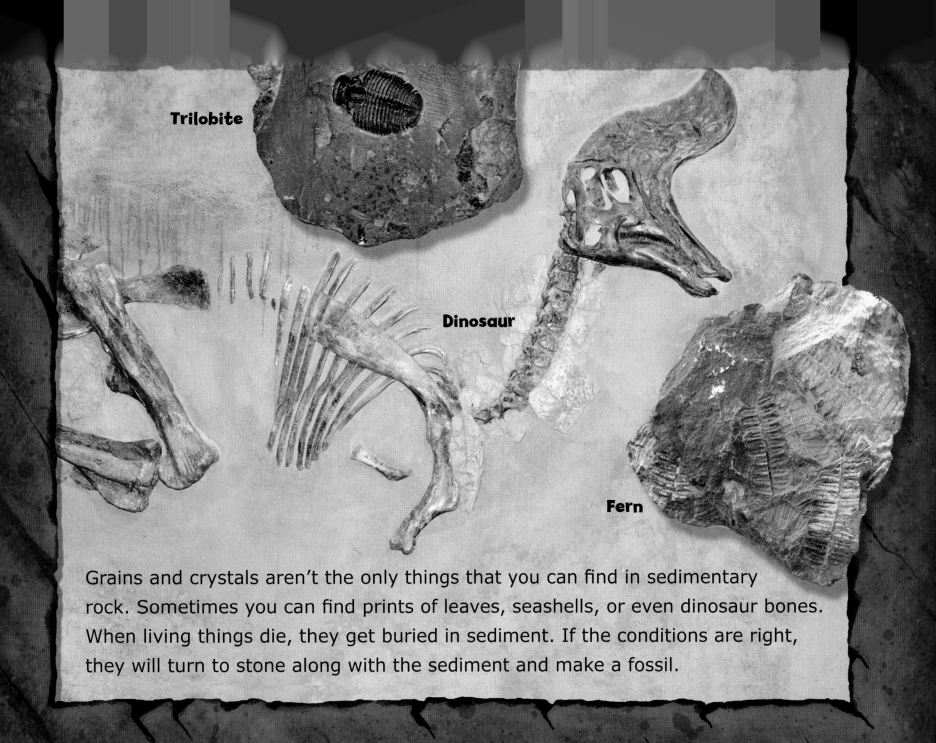

Trilobite

Dinosaur

Fern

Grains and crystals aren't the only things that you can find in sedimentary rock. Sometimes you can find prints of leaves, seashells, or even dinosaur bones. When living things die, they get buried in sediment. If the conditions are right, they will turn to stone along with the sediment and make a fossil.

The Rock Cycle

Rocks on our Earth are always changing. In some places wind and water wear rocks away. In other places lava from volcanoes brings new rocks to the Earth's surface.

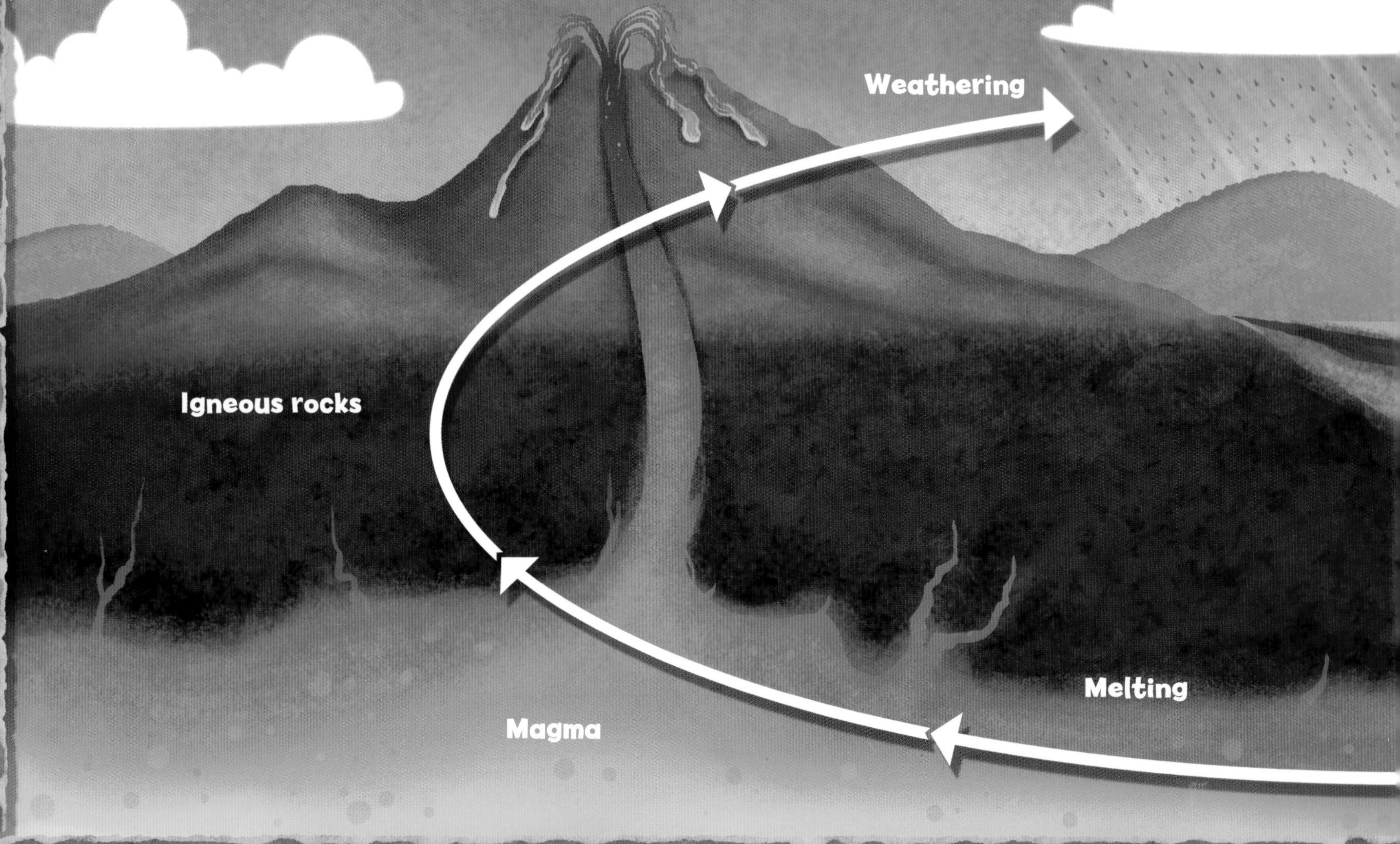

Weathering

Igneous rocks

Melting

Magma

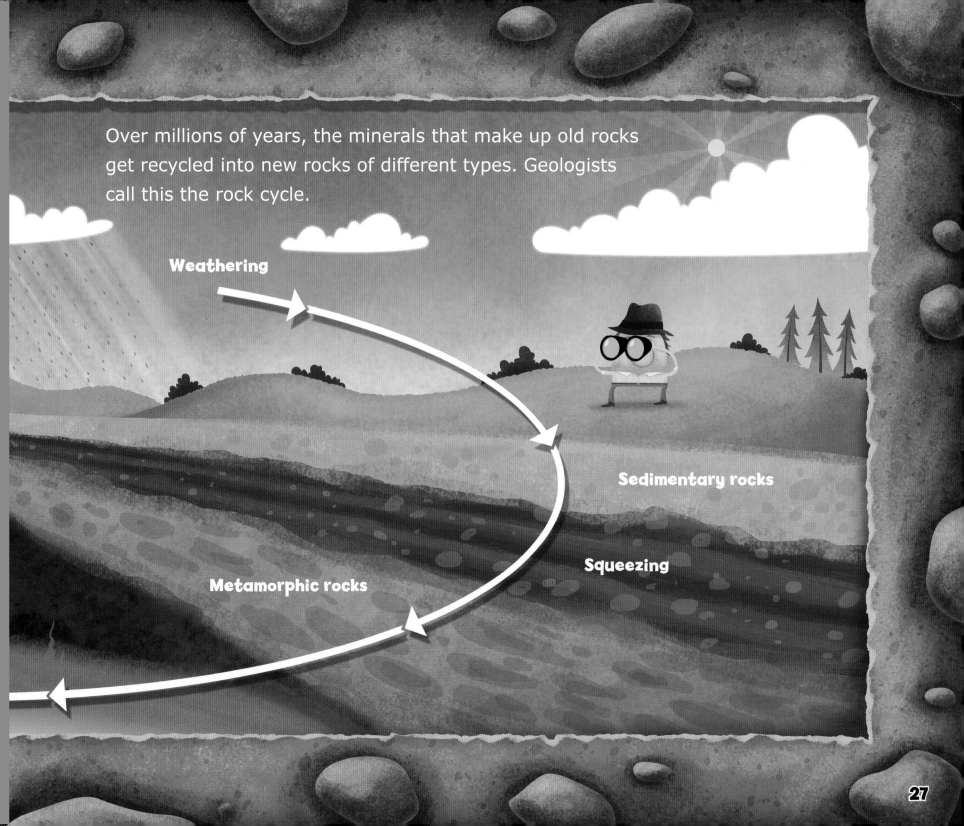

Over millions of years, the minerals that make up old rocks get recycled into new rocks of different types. Geologists call this the rock cycle.

Weathering

Sedimentary rocks

Squeezing

Metamorphic rocks

Rocks are all around us. They form in different ways and they have many uses. The minerals that make up rocks have many different properties and you can use those properties to help tell them apart.

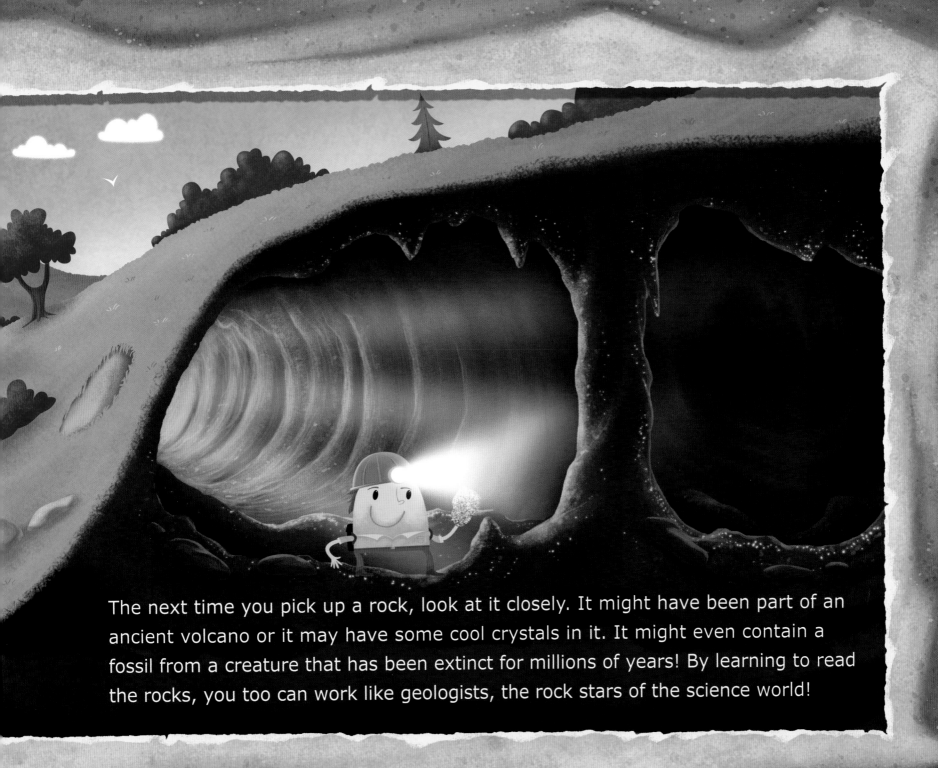

The next time you pick up a rock, look at it closely. It might have been part of an ancient volcano or it may have some cool crystals in it. It might even contain a fossil from a creature that has been extinct for millions of years! By learning to read the rocks, you too can work like geologists, the rock stars of the science world!

Making a Rock at Home

You can design your own rock using some simple materials.

Here's what you'll need:

- 7 oz disposable plastic drinking cup
- large bottle of white glue
- ½ cup sand
- ½ cup pebbles
- an adult to help you

1. Pour a small amount of sand into the plastic cup so it just covers the bottom. Carefully pour white glue into the cup so all the sand is covered in glue.

2. Drop a few pebbles into the cup so they make a single layer on top of the sand. Add more glue to cover the pebbles.

3. Pour in a second layer of sand on top of the pebbles followed by another layer of glue. The cup should be about half full.

4. Place the cup in a safe place for one full week to allow the glue to dry. After a week goes by, test your rock by poking at the top of it. If the glue is still soft, allow it to dry for a few more days.

5. Once the glue is hard, carefully peel away the plastic cup from the mixture inside. If some of the glue is still wet, wipe it off with a damp paper towel. What type of rock have you created?

1

2

3

4

5

What did you discover?
(use a mirror to read)

The rock you made is a sedimentary rock called a conglomerate (see page 13) because it is made of sand and pebbles mixed together. The sediment you used is the same kind of sediment that might be carried by a stream into a lake or ocean. The glue is like the natural cement that is carried by water flowing underground. When the glue is completely dry, it should almost disappear, so all you have left is a homemade sedimentary rock with the grains stuck together. Try making several other types of sedimentary rocks using different kinds of sediment.

Published by the National Geographic Society.
Reproduction of the whole or any part of the contents
without written permission from the publisher is prohibited.

The National Geographic Society is one of the world's largest non-profit scientific and educational organizations. Founded in 1888 to "increase and diffuse geographic knowledge," the Society works to inspire people to care about the planet. National Geographic reflects the world through its magazines, television programs, films, music and radio, books, DVDs, maps, exhibitions, live events, school publishing programs, interactive media and merchandise. *National Geographic* magazine, the Society's official journal, published in English and 32 local-language editions, is read by more than 35 million people each month. The National Geographic Channel reaches 310 million households in 34 languages in 165 countries. National Geographic Digital Media receives more than 13 million visitors a month. National Geographic has funded more than 9,200 scientific research, conservation and exploration projects and supports an education program promoting geography literacy. For more information, visit nationalgeographic.com.

For more information, please call 1-800-NGS LINE (647-5463)
or write to the following address:
National Geographic Society
1145 17th Street N.W.
Washington, D.C. 20036-4688 U.S.A.

Visit us online at www.nationalgeographic.com/books

For librarians and teachers: www.ngchildrensbooks.org

More for kids from National Geographic: kids.nationalgeographic.com

For information about special discounts for bulk purchases,
please contact National Geographic Books Special Sales:
ngspecsales@ngs.org

For rights or permissions inquiries, please contact
National Geographic Books Subsidiary Rights:
ngbookrights@ngs.org

Photo credits

Cover, 1, 2 (polished rocks) Karol Kozlowski/ Shutterstock; (minerals) dmitriyd/ Shutterstock; (amethyst geode) Aaron Haupt/ Photo Researchers, Inc.; (gemstones) Susan S. Carroll/ Shutterstock; 8 (top left), Charles D. W inters/Photo Researchers, Inc.; 8 (bottom left), R. Mackay Photogtaphy, LLC/ Shutterstock; 8 (bottom center), E. R. Degginger/ Photo Researchers, Inc.; 8 (right center), Igor Kaliuzhnyi/ Shutterstock; 8 (top right), Susan S. Carroll/ Shutterstock; 8 (bottom right), Arturo Limon/ Shutterstock; 8 (top center), Jiri Slama/ Shutterstock; 9 (top left), Manamana/ Shutterstock; 9 (bottom left), Lawrence Lawry/ Photo Researchers, Inc.; 9 (top center), Charles D. Winters/ Photo Researchers, Inc.; 9 (bottom center), goldenangel/ Shutterstock; 9 (bottom right), Ted Kinsman/ Photo Researchers, Inc.; 9 (top right), Gontar/ Shutterstock; 10 (top left), Brian Brockman/ Shutterstock; 10 (bottom right), Carolina K. Smith, M.D./ Shutterstock; 10 (top right), Wellford Tiller/ Shutterstock; 10 (bottom left), Jose Gil/ Shutterstock; 11 (top), dibrova/ Shutterstock; 11 (center), Phillip Minnis/ Shutterstock; 11 (bottom), Vicente Barcelo Varona/ Shutterstock; 12 (left), Dirk Wiersma/ Photo Researchers, Inc.; 12 (right), Ted Kinsman/ Photo Researchers, Inc.; 13, John R. Foster/ Photo Researchers, Inc.; 15 (top), A. B. Joyce/ Photo Researchers, Inc.; 15 (bottom), Dirk Wiersma/ Photo Researchers, Inc.; 17, Trevor Clifford Photography/ Photo Researchers, Inc.; 19 (top), Biophoto Associates/ Photo Researchers, Inc.; 19 (bottom), Joel Arem/ Photo Researchers, Inc.; 24 (inset), Peter J. Kovacs/ Shutterstock; 25 (top), Tim Illencik/ Shutterstock; 25 (center), B.G. Smith/ Shutterstock; 25 (right), Tom Grundy/ Shutterstock; 32, (polished rocks) Karol Kozlowski/ Shutterstock; 32, (minerals) dmitriyd/ Shutterstock; 32, (amethyst geode) Aaron Haupt/ Photo Researchers, Inc.; 32, (gemstones) Susan S. Carroll/ Shutterstock.

Library of Congress Cataloging-in-Publication Data

Tomecek, Steve.
Jump into science: rocks and minerals / by Steve Tomecek;
illustrated by Kyle Poling
    p. cm.
 ISBN 978-1-4263-0538-2 (hardcover: alk. paper)—
 ISBN 978-1-4263-0539-9 (lib. bdg.: alk. paper
1. Rocks—Juvenile literature. 2. Minerals—Juvenile literature.
I. Poling, Kyle, ill. II. Title.
 QE432.2.T66 2010
 552--dc22

Printed in China
10/RRDS/1